A Homesteader's Year on Deer Isle

A Homesteader's Year on Deer Isle

by Anneli Carter-Sundqvist

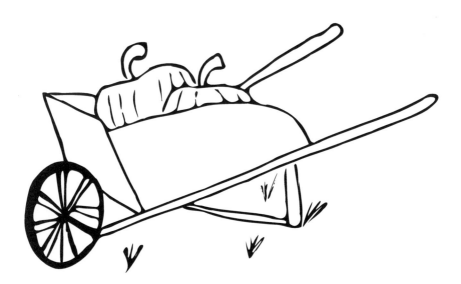

Deer Isle Hostel and Homestead ~ Deer Isle, Maine

Graphic layout and cover design© George Eaton

Cover photos ©
Cabbage head; Hostel entrance; Watering can; Hostel with garden; Dennis
and Anneli: Layla Motta
Lumber; Hostel Building in winter; Peaches; Peach blossom: Anneli Carter-
Sundqvist
Baby chick; Piglets: Jennifer Cronborn
Sunflower; Colleen M. Delaney

Inside photos ©
Photo # 7, 8, 9: Layla Motta
All other photos: Anneli Carter-Sundqvist & Dennis Carter

Illustrations ©
Anneli Carter-Sundqvist

ISBN: 978-0-578-13833-6

Published by Deer Isle Hostel and Homestead
For sales and trade distribution, please contact
Anneli Carter-Sundqvist
65 Tennis Rd
Deer Isle, ME

207-348-2308 ~ info@deerislehostel.com
www.deerislehostel.com

Today I'm thankful for...

*the wildest winter weather in many years that allowed for the
chance to put this book together. I'm also thankful for
Anne and Peter Beerits who let me
use their jelly-kitchen as my writing studio
and for Sue Newlin and Olive Savage
who took on the daunting task
of cleaning up my English grammar.
And for George and Hannah, who not only read the
texts and did all the graphic work but more than
anything, believed in this project from the first moment.
And I'm thankful for Dennis – my best friend – for making space in
our lives so I could spend the time doing this.*

Introduction

When I as a kid dreamed about what to do with my life, homesteading never crossed my mind. I came from Sweden to America for the first time in 2005, to drive a car through what I perceived as the outrageous south, aiming for the wild west coast. In my early 20s, Maine, from a distance, seemed pretty dull.

Still here's where I ended up a few years later. Dennis and I met in the south of Georgia at a hostel and a year later my travels around the world brought me back to the US, and this time to Deer Isle. Not even then did I think I would actually stay, not even then did I think of homesteading as something I would do as a way of living.

In 2009 we opened the Hostel in a 17th Century inspired timber framed house that Dennis built from the granite foundation up, on the same land as our much smaller cabin. As the years passed I found myself extending my visa over and over and somewhere along the line I started to think about this as a long-term commitment. Eventually Dennis and I got married and I could stay in the country permanently, settling in to the rhythm of living off the land and running a hostel.

A homesteader's year is in some aspects similar from one year to the next. I plant the garden in the spring and harvest it in the fall. In our case, we run the Hostel in the summers and we do forestry in the winters. As we develop our skills and thoughts on various matters, engage in new projects or try other ways of doing things, the years will also be very different. The texts are blogs I wrote and published on *Mother Earth News'* website as a way to paint a picture of our lives at present rather than to tell a story about one specific year.

A keen reader will notice that some thoughts around how and why we do things here come back throughout the book. It's inevitable, since what we do here is all interconnected. Our strive for self-reliance and independence influences us on a daily basis, in almost every aspect of what we're doing, so does our connection to nature. The homestead is for us to live from, but also for the Hostel guests to enjoy. The garden is a part of our livelihood, but also a part of our educational program. Our work in the woods is integrated with our food production in many ways, for example that we keep the produce in boxes made from spruce boards, packed in sawdust we get as we mill the lumber. By giving our animals damaged and diseased fruit from the orchard we both feed our livestock from a backyard resource and promote better health for the trees. Our appreciation for natural materials is connected to our desire to live in a natural setting.

Whether you already live as a homesteader, have the ambition to someday do so or whether you live a whole different life quite happily, I hope and believe you'll find something in these texts to take with you while walking this planet. Enjoy the read, and enjoy the walk!

My Exotic Daily Life

Winter is a time for me to visit family and friends in my old hometown Umeå in the north of Sweden. A city of 110,000 inhabitants, friends and siblings, all of whom have lives similar to the one I once had – before Maine, before Deer Isle, long before I'd even heard the word homesteading. Lives with careers and mortgages, lives where smart is a phone, sourdough bread a fashion and organic, locally grown produce makes people like you on Facebook.

I have left the cities I once called home, I have left houses with radiant heat, apartments with rent and appliances. Kitchen taps with warm water, convenient 3-minute showers, outlets with unlimited power in every corner of every room, daily newspapers, daily commute, daily grind.

It wasn't for the opportunity to rack up my exoticism credits that I chose a small homestead on an island in Maine. Still my everyday life, the chores and the repetitive routines becomes for others something extremely fascinating. How many people get to explain how they keep their food cold, when talking about what they do nowadays?

Every summer we open our home to hundreds of Hostel guests, many of whom come straight from the city and seem to take their first hesitant steps outside a flat, paved driveway when arriving at our place – wide eyes, a sense of adventure. I appreciate the interest shown in my life and in a more sustainable, conscientious way of living.

"How big is this island again?" someone asked me. Three thousand residents in winter and about six thousand in the summer. "And you only have solar power?" Yes, only solar power. "Do you have a phone?" Yes, we need the phone for the Hostel. But no cell phone. Up until a year ago almost no one I knew had a cell phone. No one expects me to have one, and I would never remember to carry it with me. A moment of silence usually follows, to contemplate this vast unknown: a place where cell phones aren't expected.

I met one of my oldest Swedish friends the other day, she confided in me that she and her partner had bought a house in the mountains, without running water. She needed advice. Well, I explained, we have a bucket in the kitchen with drinking water and a bucket under the sink to catch the dish water. A hand pump outside the house. All this is pretty normal by now; fill up the bucket and bring it in. I don't feel exotic, or radical or anything. It's just about the same feeling most get when turning on the tap. Just something they do. "How do you heat the water?" my friend wanted to know. On the wood stove, I said. Just put the water on the stove. "How do you take baths?" she said. I explained that in the summer we use an outdoor shower and a watering can that we fill with warm water and hoist up with a rope and pulley. In the winter we use a rubber tub on the kitchen floor. We heat the water, bathe, and empty the tub outside. It kinda' gobbles up the evening, between my bath and my husband's, but that's what we do. "Like how often?" she said and couldn't hide that look people get on safaris when approaching a newly discovered tribal society in a remote part of Africa. "Once a week?" and I almost expected her to whip out a camera when I nodded "Yes."

And we heat with wood and cook with wood. We mill our own lumber, and go out in the forest when we need building material: that tree and that one for the frame, those for the roof, those for the walls.

We don't go to the store. Well, we do go for soap and toilet paper and an occasional bottle of wine, but otherwise all the meat, egg, fruit and veggies we could possibly eat are to be found in the gardens, the orchard and the root cellar. The fact that we raise pigs and butcher them ourselves is met with great curiosity, as is the occasional deer we come across and the abundance of clams to dig. We trade produce for dairy products, such as cheese and yogurt and sometimes tomato seedlings for a pound of coffee. "Like the old times," my friend laughed and warmed my heart in the cold Swedish winter evening. Indeed, as the old times. Or the new times, depending on your point of view. Exotic or not, if people like it, it's great. If they dare to try, it's even better. I don't mind answering the questions.

8000 Square Feet of Garden in a Box

I made it back from Sweden just in time to be snowed in by the worst blizzard this winter. Here I was met by perhaps the most exciting mail delivery of the year: the seed order. It wasn't many months ago the seed catalog for this year showed up, but at that point I had just managed to finish off the garden season and was slightly traumatized from all the work. To receive a catalog at that point seemed like an ill-conceived joke, a way to rub it in: "Don't think you can relax too much. Soon spring will be here again." I hid the catalog on the messy bookshelf and forgot I had ever seen it.

And now the seeds are here. Somewhere between now and then I must have pulled myself together, sent in the order and quickly hidden the catalog again. I wasn't ready, not yet. Like hitting snooze on the alarm. Just a few more minutes.

Last year took me by surprise. Snuck up on me and not necessarily stabbed me in the back, but it did startle me. I cultivated an even larger area than in previous years, dealt with an unseen amount of pests and put away more food than ever for the winter. On top of that, the Hostel grew twice as big as the year before. So what's new about hard work? Nothing, of course. It's a part of life, if you choose this life. But I, I wasn't ready for it. I bobbed with my head just above the surface from April until December. Surely I had a lot of fun and rewards along the way, but man oh man, I was so ready for it to end.

After growing up in a place with distinct differences between summer (never ending daylight) and winter (almost complete darkness) and now living off the land where the year also is clearly divided into four seasons, I have developed a deeply rooted appreciation for the kind of life that those differences offer. As soon as the winter lets go, we're at it. Non-stop. Prune the fruit trees, prepare the garden beds. Plant the first cold hardy seeds, start the tomato seedlings and pepper plants. The pace picks up as the days grow longer. A wild roar carries us into summer, to planting all those seedlings, mulching all the beds, thinning those first plants.

Suddenly we have to mow the grass and just as suddenly we can eat the first carrots, the first early broccoli. We chase the bugs, the raccoons, the deer, the crows. Our piglets show up in the middle of all

11

this and the Hostel guests come to see what we're up to. We carry water, seaweed, buckets of compost. We celebrate the bounty, the summer, our life in general. Suddenly the whole garden explodes in a crescendo of ripe food that needs to be dealt with: stored, dried, fermented or canned. For a while is seems it will never end. We build tower after tower of boxes full of root crops in the cellar, line the shelves with pickles and kraut and apple sauce and pear sauce.

Then slowly, just as unexpected as spring was nine months ago, the end will come. One day, my "to do" list will be so pathetic I won't even care to write it any more. Perhaps I'll cheat and not cut those last dry stalks in the flower bed or decide to wait until spring to turn the compost pile. Enough is enough. Winter comes as a kind friend every year, timely, just as we finish off all the outdoor chores. Long mornings, the slowly coming daylight. Early darkness in the afternoons. There are trees to fell and lumber to mill, but all at our own pace. Books to read, mittens to knit. Time to see our friends, those who are also too busy to socialize in the summer, those who actually stay here when all the summer visitors have left. Those who are our neighbors, our community.

It's late January and all this is behind us and ahead of us at the same time. Our house is still full of food from last year, and the box of seeds sits there on the kitchen table. The box is smaller than the average pie pumpkin but big as a rutabaga, as a couple of mason jars of pickled beans, and it holds an 8000 square-foot garden and food for a whole year. Today, I feel like I can do it. The whole cycle over again. No, I don't only feel like I can do it, I feel like it will be fun, really fun. My hands in the dirt, the moist soil, the first emerging sprouts. The fresh greens to harvest, the sun ripe tomatoes. The time for rest is almost behind us as the sun climbs a bit higher each day. The cycle takes a new turn and I can sense a light tingle of itching to get out there again. Bring on the spring, bring on the new garden year. I'm ready for it to start.

Small-Scale Forestry for the Homestead

Winter lends itself nicely to working in the woods, and it's one of my favorite things to do around the homestead. It's great to be outside with the ax, the chain saw or the pole saw enjoying the sparkling snow and thinking about the generations after us that also will have trees, beauty and wildlife to enjoy. Forestry at the homestead, or the part of it where we fell trees, is fundamentally different from the kind of commercial logging operations that strip acre after acre bare of everything alive.

First of all, forestry on a sustainable scale is often talked about as "low impact," but I rather think of it as "positive impact." While the grade of impact isn't without importance, "low" sometimes is mistaken for not touching it at all while "positive," to me, suggests that our work always contributes to the long-term health, beauty and usability of the woods. Positive-impact forestry helps the woods to sustain itself and all life forms in it, including humans. It helps balance the competition among species, it creates adequate sunlight for new and healthy growth, it encourages wildlife by supporting trees and shrubs that provide feed and it helps manage the water supply.

We live on a 16-acre parcel of land that pretty much was clear cut in the 1940s and grew back largely as white spruce and balsam fir, neither of which is our first choice for lumber and firewood. Rather, these fast-growing but short-lived species quickly out compete what for us would be more useful varieties.

Our work in the woods starts long before we get the chainsaw and ax out, merely by being out there to observe and contemplate. We are looking for healthy trees that we can help to thrive and that will be beneficial both to us and their surroundings in the future. We like to promote what red spruce population we do have because of its longevity and value as a building material, so we're trying to reduce competition around them. We also like to promote oak trees, whose acorns can feed both wildlife and our pigs, and we also like to support the apple trees that dot the woods around here, again a substantial source of sustenance.

Next we clear trails and roads to the area we decide to work in, and then we fell dead trees so we can walk around and see what's actually standing there that might be worth favoring. We use a human-powered log arch – a piece of equipment that causes virtually no damage on the ground – to move the logs. With the log arch Dennis, a helper and I together can move up to 800-pound logs quite a distance.

We don't cut any living trees unless we have a need and a purpose for them, and we don't fell more trees than we can process before they rot. If we intend to mill the logs we need to have the time it takes and we need to know we will be able to get the mill to the trees or the trees to the mill. The parts of the trees not suitable for milling are cut up for firewood and used for heating and cooking. We have several oaks around our yard that should be thinned out to allow for more sunlight for the gardens, but those oaks would provide perfect logs for timber framing so we have decided to leave them until we're ready for a project like that.

At all times when working in the woods I keep in mind that most of those trees have been there for a very long time or ultimately would be there for a long time. It might not even take a minute to fell something that's been standing longer than I have been around, but once it's down, it's down. Look twice, cut once, but only if necessary. Enjoy winter!

Start Your Onions from Seed

The garden season has begun, with the first sprouted seed. Indoors, of course, since outdoors still will be covered in snow for weeks to come. A Copra onion, planted on the 13th of February, now grows in a tray on our kitchen table. With equal amounts of care and luck, this tiny little seedling will be planted outside in April, harvested in August, and still will be good to eat in June of next year.

We used to plant our onions from sets. We bought the nondescript bulbs at the store and planted them when the time was right. They never failed, but they never blew us away either. Well, over the last few years as we have produced and stored almost all of the food we eat, we have also changed the way we raise onions. With the aspiration of being onion self-sufficient, starting them from seed is our best option since it allows us to be more specific about what kinds to grow. After a few years of experimenting, we've pretty much settled on Copra for our storage onions and Alisa Craig – a mild and sweet onion, perfect for hot summer day meals – as our August treat.

Last year we ran out of onions in June, and they had kept perfectly. Two months later, in August, we harvested a thousand onions. I know, I know. It got out of hand. Who eats a thousand onions over the course of a single year? Well, we do, almost. Three meals a day – baked, cooked, fried, pickled, fresh. And if we can't go through them all, we can trade them for something else. If you can keep it, you can eat it, all year long.

Onions are daylight sensitive and need to have plenty of time to put on top growth before the days start to get shorter again and the plants begin to put their energy into the bulb. If you like to start onions from seed, don't wait! The best time is already closing in. Our house has a big, south-facing window, and even though it sometimes gets down into the low 50s at night, the onions sprouted after only a few days. They will grow as dense as a lawn, and as they get taller I trim the tops down to a about three inches (those can be sprinkled over a salad or roasted veggies for a chive-like flavoring). As soon as possible we plant them outside. Last year we transplanted the seedlings on the 21st of April. We use any simple tool to make a small, two inches deep furrow across the well-fed bed and then we place the grass-straw like plants three inches apart and scuff the dirt with our hands so they stand upright. We then move forward about twelve inches and make another furrow. We find that distance between furrows works best for us as less space makes it hard to put the seaweed mulch down between the rows.

But all that is still far away: April, mulching, spreading compost. It's still only the end of February and another blizzard is upon us. How sweet it is to sit here and look out over winter while eating last summer's harvest with the plate only inches away from next summer's crop.

Extending Our Season with Recycled Cold Frames

We've reached the point of no return: the new season is starting. The gardens, the farm, the Hostel, the everything. There's no end now until December and I'm ready and I'm excited.

Next, after starting the onions, come the Brassicas. Though many varieties in the Brassica family can be direct-seeded later in the season and do just fine, I find there are several advantages to starting them earlier in a warm space. A 6-8-week head start before transplanting them outside will make the plants better able to stand rough weather and they won't be as likely to be chewed up by slugs or flea beetles. Some Brassica, as different kinds of broccoli and cauliflower, are short-seasoned, and if started in March they can be enjoyed in July.

I raise several hundred broccoli, cauliflower, cabbage and Brussels sprout seedlings for us and for trading with friends and family. Our kitchen table already is compromised by the trays of onions, so this past week we built new cold frames in which to start all those seedlings. A cold frame is a box without a bottom that sits on the ground with a glass lid. The glass creates a warm environment either for starting plants early in the spring or for planting cold-hardy greens late in the fall, leaving them there to over-winter for spring treats.

Our cold frame glass panes have a long legacy of famous homesteaders and gardeners: they once belonged to Eliot Coleman, an organic grower and author of the book *Four Season Harvest* who lives on Cape Rosier, Maine. The cold frames were then moved next door, to the Good Life Center. That was originally the home of pioneer homesteaders Scott and Helen Nearing, whom many credit with the "back to the land" movement of the 1960s. They lived in Maine the last part of their lives, a story captured in one of their many books, *The Good Life*.

We have a lot of reasons not to use plastic as a way of extending our season. For one, we live in a place put together by wood, metal and glass, and plastic doesn't appeal to us aesthetically. Also, glass good enough to grow plants under is easy for us to find; our small town dump always has stacks of used windows free for the taking. Coming

17

across greenhouse-quality plastic is harder, especially if you're looking for a greenhouse-sized piece.

Season-extending materials made from plastic have gained incredible popularity in the world of organic and sustainable gardening even though it's totally dependent on fossil fuel. I don't see how that could be sustainable, but the argument usually is that there's less fossil fuel used in the making of the greenhouse materials than there is in the transport of lettuce from a warmer climate to colder Maine. That may be true, but there are several ways of enjoying fresh salads every day, in all seasons, without modern, oil-dependent materials *or* transportation. We still have fresh cabbage in our root cellar that I shred and mix with carrots or beets and different fermented vegetables. Any day now I can harvest the kale and spinach I planted last fall in our simple glass and wood cold frames. We have closed the circle: fresh salad from our own garden twice a day, year round. If we didn't have free, recycled material from which to build the frames, I could probably start a tray of spinach and claytonia on our kitchen table in front of our south-facing window. Or I could harvest early wild greens, such as dandelion leaves and spruce buds or, as a last resort, live without fresh greens for a couple of months and eat the vegetables we still have in the cellar and really, truly enjoy the first lettuce leaves only as you enjoy something long missed.

Dead Trees Full of Life

When thinking about forestry and what we do in the woods, it's easy to think only about the living things: the spruce to save for lumber, the oak and maple that will heat our house, how to thin a stand, prune a stand, cut a stand. But the value of dead wood for forest health and vigor should not be overlooked.

It seems paradoxical, that the dead trees are bearers of so much life. From birds to bears, foxes to fishers and from fungi to insects and bacteria: all need the dead wood for food and shelter. These different life forms are what keep the woods healthy by decomposing the organic matter which adds to the nutrients in the ground and provides a habitat for new seeds to sprout. Logs and brush on the ground help balance the water supply and prevent soil erosion.

This past week I worked in an area previously untouched by us, predominantly just a stand of dead fir trees. Beyond it was a beautiful stretch of red spruce, trees that can provide building material for many years to come. By removing the dead trees we now have a way to get to the spruce trees and a path in which to fell them, while at the same time allowing for sunlight and preventing blow downs that could make the work of cutting the spruce harder and more dangerous.

"Cleaning up" dead trees can be done in many ways, but should always be done with consideration and thoughtfulness. Forests in an untouched, healthy stage will keep the ground covered with leaves, twigs and mosses; some trees will be standing dead and logs will be decaying on the ground, all of it a part of the natural life cycle. There's no reason for us humans to change that; we should leave forest debris on the ground as we leave organic matter in our garden. It will break down and become nutrients for the trees and plants that in turn will support and benefit other life forms: birds, mammals, fungi and eventually, us. We provide habitats for animals in the woods by leaving dead standing trees just as we provide habitats for animals in our yard by putting up for example a birdhouse.

When we cut dead trees around here we almost always leave them right where they fell, moving only what we need to keep paths and roads clear. And no matter how we try, we won't ever cut all of them out as there are just too many. As we have expanded our clearing to establish gardens and orchards, we've stacked brush and dead logs in a long mound along the edge of the woods. It blends in to the background forest, it frames our yard nicely and it provides hiding places and habitats for all kinds of wildlife. As the years pass, the brush will decompose and sink into the ground, becoming nutrients that support new life.

To turn a woodlot into a park with no "litter" on the ground might look tidy, but is not very healthy or functional. To me "pretty" is something that is natural and serves benefit to many life forms, as the dead and dying trees are. Now when I look at a dead tree or a log rotting on the ground, what I see is something full of life.

Homesteading Economics 101

  I split and stacked three cords of firewood this past week and it made for some long days, indeed. Whenever I needed some encouragement, I repeated to myself what I heard on the radio the other day: the average Maine household will spend $4,000 on heating oil this year. That, I can tell you straight up, is more than Dennis and I will profit from the Hostel this summer.

For a number of years we have made some choices that now enable us to live with a very limited need for money, much less than most people. One of the most important factors for this freedom from money is that neither of us carries any debt. Our land is paid for and so are our student loans. We've spent a couple of years investing time and labor in our farm; we have established gardens and orchards big enough to support us through the year and we're raising pigs and improving on how to feed them off our land. We trade things that we produce, such as squash and onions, for things we don't produce, such as goat cheese and coffee. We have built adequate outbuildings – a chicken house, a wood shed and a smoke house – and we have invested in tools and equipment to provide our own lumber and granite for building materials. We do all the maintenance on our car, bikes and utility trailer; and we invest time in learning how to do all this.

In the spring, summer and fall, I go to work once a week landscaping in the neighborhood and in late winter I prune apple trees for a week or so. I appreciate leaving my own yard once in a while: it's a great chance to pick up outside inspiration and skills to use at home. It amounts to about 35-40 days of work off the farm each year. And that, my friends, is enough. Dennis and I have chosen to spend our life together; therefore we like to spend our days together. We have chosen this place to live; therefore we like to spend most of our days here.

I see it as a circle: we provide our own needs at home, which minimizes our need to work for money, which in turn allows us to spend the time improving on how to meet our needs at home, from the gardens and the woods. The cash we do make from the Hostel we invest back in it with the goal of growing it to a point where one day it will support us financially.

I appreciate the low-cash life we now live. Money, to me, often is used as a shortcut: if you can buy your way to what you want, your own skills matter less and connections and a community for trading and helping hands lose their value. Creativity and problem solving is replaced with the far too common "I want it now" attitude.

Homesteading has many political reasons: one being the desire to stay as far away as possible from the general financial system. Money comes with questions about ethics and morality. As a wage earner, I need to ask myself who pays me and how the individual or business I'm working for has made its money. As a consumer it's my responsibility to question what the consequences of my purchases are. What resources got used in manufacturing and transporting, what human lives were impacted and who really benefited from my spending the money.

A low-cash life equals freedom. Even if we have a business at home that through the summer meets our year-round need for money, I want that need to be minimal. Then the summers will be ours to enjoy the Hostel and all its guests, but also to have time for canoe rides and hikes and swims in the pond. If we keep making choices to live without a lot of things that would cost money to get, do or maintain, not only the summers, but our entire year, our whole lives will be ours to use creativity, skills and ingenuity to meet our needs.

Milling the Homestead Necessities

A few years ago a major piece of our homesteading puzzle fell into place when we bought a Wood-Mizer portable sawmill. Up to that point we'd been dependent on the lumber yard and its supply, as well as friends and acquaintances with occasional stacks of lumber for us to riffle through or logs to mill somewhere else. Because we don't have any heavy equipment to transport logs with, anything cut on our land had to be moved by someone else, first to a mill and then back here.

Now, on every first day of a new building project we start where all building projects ought to start: in the woods. We select the trees that fit our intended purpose, fell them, haul them with our people-powered log hauler and turn them into lumber right here in our yard. Last year we built a timber-framed hut from a red oak that started to shade the garden; that entire frame didn't travel more than 300 feet from the stump to the mill to the site.

But not all logs have to come to our yard. The mill isn't so big or heavy that it can't be loaded onto our trailer and hauled behind our Subaru. This week we have the Wood-Mizer set up a couple of miles down the road at a friend's place. He's a tree feller and has stacked up a pile of cedar, black locust and spruce – really nice red spruce – that's all ours as a trade for milling the hardwood for him. We get the perfect lumber for our next projects and he gets the perfectly matched lumber for the sauna he'll build at his place.

We bought the portable mill to provide our own building material and to make use of the trees that need to come down around our yard. The gasoline it takes to run the machine is a tradeoff, but for us the gains are so many that the emission footprint still is much smaller than it would have been if we had to go somewhere to buy what we now can produce. In addition, the by-products have turned out to be just as valuable to us as the lumber. For one thing, the sawmill gives us slabs (the off cuts with bark on one side). Tons of slabs and for anyone cooking on a small wood stove, there's nothing better to get your tea water boiling than some dry spruce slabs. We get enough for ourselves, and then more. We give slabs to neighbors and friends and in return we get something else, like warm spaces to start tomato seedlings in or help to look after our chickens if we go away somewhere.

Then there's the sawdust. It might not sound like much compared with the $1,000 pieces of locust we cut this morning, but I don't know what we would do without the sawdust the milling provides us. I don't know what we did before we had the mill as we use the sawdust in our outhouses, to pack the root crops in for storage and in our chicken house. We go through perhaps 60 feed sacks of it every year, a resource we would have to go somewhere to get if it weren't for our mill. To say the sawmill is a piece in the homesteading puzzle might be a slight understatement as in some ways it's a key factor. It enables us to progress with our building projects without necessarily having the money it otherwise would take, it ties us to our community with labor- and resource trades, and it makes it easier for us to store food, keep our chicken house clean and have nice outhouses for the Hostel guests. Some of the essence of homesteading right there: providing for yourself and your community using your own resources and making the most of what's around you. Who would ever have thought that a Wood-Mizer would to the trick?

The Homesteaders' Vehicles

It's late April and the roads on the island are getting increasingly busy. While the snow plows have been put away for the year, the lobster boats are about to be hauled to the harbor and the main street in town soon will go from being deserted to traffic-jammed. Out-of-state cars will appear and everything will take off from there: delivery trucks, carpentry crews, landscaping crews, trailers and campers.

Through all this, through all seasons, Dennis and I ride our bikes. Through all this, through all seasons, Dennis and I are among the few, the very few, actually, on this island of 3000 year-round residents, who use our bikes to do errands. There are those who ride for leisure or exercise, but with a bike bag to the hardware store? Almost no one, but us. The 3-mile stretch to the village takes me to the coffee shop, the post office and the pond for summer dips. Even in the spring, with snow-free roads, that ride is enough to almost garner me a round of applause. The 9-mile one-way route to the island's bigger town takes me by the chain-saw store, the library and the Inn with its sundeck for afternoon down time. That trip is enough to be greeted as a hero. Once a year I go on my bike to the Maine Organic Farmers and Gardeners fair, which is 75 miles from here. It's a very pleasant day's ride through an interior part of Maine I never otherwise see. For people here at home I might as well set out on the *Tour de France.*

I love bikes and I love riding them. Growing up in Sweden, it was a part of every kid's life, as it was for most adults as well, to have a bike. If you had a bike, your freedom to move around was boundless. Bikes are swift, easy to navigate where cars sometimes can't go, they are cheap and they are quiet. You can listen to the birds and you see things you easily could miss from a car. Sometimes I take my bike down the same old road I've gone in a car hundreds of times and it's like I've never been there before.

Unfortunately, the conditions for bike riding here on the island are far from perfect: the roads don't have shoulders to distance bikers from the passing cars, the drivers are often heedless and impatient. Still, I rode my bike year round through the much bigger cities where I lived in Sweden, bike lanes or not. A lot of people here commute short distances with their cars; perhaps it's habit, culture or a narrow view of what is considered possible. Does one dare to believe, that if more people used a bike for transportation, the conditions would improve?

Sometimes people ask if we even own a car. Well, as much as we prefer our bikes, we still need the car. The farm requires materials to be moved, and we have reasons to go further than our bikes easily can carry us. But instead of having a big pick-up to go everywhere in, or one big pick-up as a farm vehicle and a smaller car for personal trips, we have a gas-efficient Subaru and a home-built utility trailer we can hitch and unhitch as needed. This gives us the cheap car we need to move around with when a car is necessary, and a farm vehicle that doesn't add any extra costs for insurance or inspections. Between the Subaru and the trailer, we can haul all that's necessary to haul: logs, seaweed, lumber, gravel, wood chips. We even can haul our portable sawmill, which would still require a trailer even if we had a pick-up truck.

So here's some advice for the coming season: see about fixing up that old bike you might have stored away somewhere. Make it nice, which will encourage you to use it. Get yourself a good helmet and a couple of bike bags and make it normal practice to bike instead of going by car. You might notice things along your own driveway you've never seen before.

Garden Expansion

My first years of homesteading here in Maine have been a lot about expanding the footprints of our gardens, so much that it has become synonymous with spring preparation. Last year was the first season I had the whole garden dug and ready with no stumps to pull and no fence to build. Boy, it is easy to plant a garden when the garden already is there.

When I first came to our homestead there was only a small garden in front of our cabin. It didn't seem small back then, but in May that year when we dug out another space just in front of the Hostel house, it seemed to dwarf the old patch. We had friends here to help us, so it was four of us digging, shoveling, raking and putting up the fence.

The second spring I doubled that garden alone. I can't remember when the decision for further expansion was made or how daunting a task I expected it to be when I first began. However, I do clearly remember how early in the mornings I had to start and how late into the evenings I was out there to have it all ready to be planted by the 1st of June. When I started, the ground was covered with stumps, rocks, brambles and weeds. We hired a guy to pull the stumps for us but had to haul them away ourselves. Then I spent about 10 days pick-axing my way through the whole God-forsaken mess before I could spend another day or so shoveling dirt from high points to low points.

Then I dug ditches. I dug so many ditches someone suggested I could count them in miles instead of numbers. I laid the 16-foot logs to make the raised beds, and I went out into the woods to find material for the fence. I'd rather not think about how it was digging the fence post holes: it was like digging to China – through clay. But I do like to think about how it felt walking down the main path through the first garden and how it was as though that path seemed to stretch forever, now that it was twice as long.

The following spring it was time again. Somewhere along the way we said we would expand the garden once more, but at least this time we had let our pigs run in the area the previous fall so the ground was broken up and the mess not quite as God-forsaken as the last time. I set out to more than double the existing size but was held up by the rainiest May we can remember, so in the end I had only a week to do it. I pick-axed out a patch big enough, quickly raked up the worst mess and planted the squash and tomatoes right there on what had been the forest floor until about a minute ago. My sister came to visit in early June, and at that point I had gone off the deep end while building the over 130-foot stretch of fence, so she and her friend finished it off. In October I finally came around to making proper planting beds and in the spring I pick-axed my way through the part that had been neither finished nor cultivated the year before. I then put up the last stretch of chicken wire and made the two gates I had left undone. For a while it seemed as if it would be hard to fill all this garden space with something, but I had worried in vain, as the space quickly was claimed: 1200 garlic, 1000 onions and potatoes for a small army of Hostelers. Soon I had to start searching for empty pockets to stick in the tomatoes, the cabbage and the corn. It's the same thing this year: so much space, so little spare room. But if I will expand the gardens soon again? This time, for sure: no.

Homesteading Economics 102

We are spending the week getting ready to open the Hostel. We're airing out mattresses and blankets, wiping kitchen counters and rehearsing the check-in procedure. Our home won't just be our home now, but a place for many to rest, eat and enjoy themselves.

Working at home can be done in many different ways. As I've mentioned before, Dennis and I do leave once in a while to make money elsewhere, but we prefer to spend our days together, at home, and produce what we need right here. For most people the word homesteading means just that: meeting basic needs at home by growing food, keeping some animals, harvesting wood, etc. For me, homesteading also means not having a great need for money and that the money we do need is being made by utilizing the land, in our case using the land as an attractive place for hostel guests to come to.

Meeting our needs at home, from the land, means that we can reap the benefits and multiply them. We could go off and make money building a shed for someone, but when we stay at home and build a hut for the Hostel, that building can make the same money year after year. It will also give us other benefits, such as further experience in timber framing, a chance to train others and an opportunity to try out various building techniques that paid work rarely allows for. Time invested in the gardens not only pays back with produce worth the equivalent of several months' pay every year, but it adds to the beauty of the farm and, again, provides training for others and a unique experience for our guests, who get to see how the dinner food was grown.

For years we've lived below the Federal poverty line, and happily so. Looking around at what we have it's hard for me to see how we by any measure could be considered poor, in the midst of this natural abundance. Our own backyard provides high-quality, organic food, material to build shelters, fuel for heating and cooking as well as recreation and beauty. If we were to work for somebody else to make the money it would take to buy what we now produce we would lose all what I consider make us rich – the connection to our land since we would leave every day, the ability to not use the car very often, the independence and the empowerment of meeting our own needs and being our own providers.

The freedom to stay at home and set our own schedule does come with challenges. To work and live in the same place means we are confronted with the work all the time, whether it's the successes, the failures or the unfinished projects. We're achievers, both Dennis and I and we love what we're doing and enjoy the hard work, traits I think most homesteaders share. I also think most of us share the experience of how easy it is to take on too much. It's all so fun and exciting, and we choose to improve, expand and add to and it's hard sometimes, to balance our ambitions with how much work feasibly can be carried out in a certain amount of time. It's a learning curve for us, to be okay with the sometimes slow pace at which it all happens and to decide *not* to expand or add to when we already have what we need.

But in the end, the choice of staying at home is easy. Believe me, I've tried many other ways: 40-hour working week, hours of commuting, sitting in an office, getting laid off when times got hard and employed when they needed another cog in the machine. I no longer want to work anywhere that means being bound to someone else's schedule, their whims of keeping me employed or customers' ability to pay. Many paying jobs also means not being fully in control over the work I'm asked to perform. I want to spend the majority of my waking time in connection to the land I reside on and with the person I love. This is my home, and here's where I should be.

Diving Into Summer

  We opened the Hostel for the season this past weekend. We're off, we're going, we're on a roll. It's happening. No bells or whistles, no fireworks, no standing ovations. Merely an acknowledgment that if anyone would call we would have to be ready to take them in. No one called. No one dropped in. No one even came by for a tour. That was all fine with me as I know from experience that before the season is over just about everyone I can handle will call, drop by or want a tour.

  Summer on Deer Isle is for me closely connected to swimming in the pond. For all the pretty coves and hidden beaches there are along the ocean, the fresh water pond is my first pick for summer soaks. Honestly, more than once I've thought, if not for the pond, I could go without summer. Too warm, too buggy, too much traffic. But if the water is warm enough to swim in, I can take the rest. Even at other times of the year I find myself visiting the oblong body of water. With its shiny ice in the winter and its bare trees in spring. It's a great place, year round, to sit down and gather my thoughts.

  The pond is still too cold to swim in, but it lingers in my thoughts, both because I long for the magical morning swims and because the image of submerging is what comes to mind as the island switches over to summer mode. From here on, everything will pick up its pace. The summer businesses will open, the year-round businesses soar, lobster boats set out each day and the carnival of out-of-state vehicles swing into motion. In my mind I see us all – Dennis and I, our friends, neighbors and community members, those we have spent the winter with and all of us who rely on the summer season for our winter needs – I see us all in union waving bye-bye to each other and with a deep breath plunging fearlessly into the Deer Isle summer. We swim and swim under the surface of all this and air bubbles rise as we try to breath slowly through our snorkels, one breath at the time, without choking. At the other end of this four-month swim we appear again and shake hands "Good job," we tell each other. "Well swum." Ahead of Dennis and me lies another Hostel season, full of guests and tours and phone calls, communal dinners, bonfires, morning coffees and check-ins and check-outs. One day, at the other end, we will sit here alone again and look back at it all wondering how it passed by so quickly.

Welcome to the Hostel!

Dennis and I live
in this cabin
year round.

Dennis built the
Hostel house from
the granite
foundation up.

Here it is in
March 2008.

In June 2009
we opened the
Deer Isle Hostel.

The Homestead

Here's where we get our water.

Inside the Hostel

This timber-framed hut was built using oak and spruce from our own land.

A good night's sleep

This is what the main garden looked like in May 2008.

In 2009 I doubled the size of the first garden.

After the 2nd expansion was done...

...I broke new ground for a yet bigger garden.

And finally it's done!

Already in February, I start the onions on our kitchen table

These cold frames are built with recycled glass and lumber from our land...

In March, I use them to start my Brassicas...

...so that we can harvest broccoli as early as July

As soon as the early potatoes are harvested, I transplant Chinese cabbage seedlings in the open space.

Carrots grown with seaweed!

We pack the root crops in boxes
with damp spruce sawdust and keep
them in our root cellar.

We store our fresh cabbage the
same way but in much bigger boxes.

Another way we preserve our produce is through fermentation, to the tune of about 30 gallons of sauerkraut...

... and hundreds of quarts of fermented beans, broccoli, corn, cucumber pickles and salsa.

Winter squash like it warm and dry, so we keep them in our former sleeping loft.

Some apples taste best in late winter after being kept in the root cellar.

Dead trees and logs left on the ground decompose and provide important nutrients for many life forms.

We stack brush in long mounds along the edge of our clearing.

With this people-powered log arch, Dennis, a helper and I together can move 800-pound logs quite a distance.

With our Wood-Mizer LT15 we cannot only produce our own lumber, but we also get many useful by-products...

...like the sawdust we use to store our root crops and as bedding for our chickens.

Pigs are scavengers and by letting them run in the woods, they fend for themselves by eating acorns and forest debris.

By butchering the pigs ourselves we can be in control over the whole process and ensure a fast and humane death for our dear animals.

At the end of the gardening season,
we cover the entire garden with seaweed.

Nothing cleans the yard as a foot of snow does,
and we get some well deserved rest...

Homesteading Education

      June is upon us and the bright nights still will get a bit brighter, the early mornings a bit earlier and the warming weather will keep getting warmer. More and more people are calling us to make their reservations for the summer. The greatest reward we can think of is to see our hard work pay off in appreciation from our Hostel guests for providing this place. Still, for the first few years of running the Hostel I often turned around after waving good-bye to our guests feeling that there ought to be more we could have given them.

Learning experiences can happen in many ways. For most, adults as well as kids, just staying as a guest at the Hostel is an eye opener: to hand pump water, having to be mindful about electricity, seeing the garden produce their dinner and to meet our pigs and our chickens. Many want more than just a brief encounter with this kind of living. It's clear to me that many people have begun to recognize the vulnerability of modern society and are now seeking to learn the skills needed to live a positive-impact, self-reliant life on whatever level they are ready to do so. We often have people – many from our own community – stopping by or giving us a call wanting to know how to prune their apple trees, what to do with their leaning barn or how to best grow their tomatoes. Young people come to us with their dreams of one day having a homestead of their own.

These encounters inspired us to start an educational program. Formal workshops, lectures and tours have their merits: we can invite others to teach, it's focused and easy to let people know it's happening. For a few years now we have offered classes focusing on the practices we use in our everyday life – long known but mostly forgotten sensible, sustainable techniques for resourcefulness and self-reliance: organic gardening, how to keep your food in a root cellar, fermentation, natural medicine, cider making and granite splitting. There's no end to the learning opportunities around our homestead.

Classes are one way to learn, but experience can come only from experiencing. That's how I got started. I came upon places similar to ours where I could stay and help out, and in that way I was introduced to an alternative way of living where hands-on labor gave the rewards of food and beauty and a connection to the land. Throughout the years a number of friends have stayed with us for longer or shorter periods of time, working alongside us in the gardens and the forest. They have experienced building the granite foundation for the Hostel house, cutting the timber frame for our new guest hut, milling lumber and harvesting produce. Last summer we took on our first formal apprentice, Megan. She sent us a letter saying she would like to learn this stuff: preserving food, gardening, working with wood. Megan turned out to be a superstar and came back in May this year to stay with us through September. We get the help we need for the season and Megan gains something she could never have gotten in a workshop: the long view. To plant the garden, weed the garden and eventually harvest, eat and preserve the produce. She gets to experience the rewards but also the inevitable routine: carrying water, picking potato bugs, emptying the composting toilet and feeding the animals. This real life experience might be the greatest asset we have to share, and it's our responsibility to do so. We live a life we believe in, in a place we will leave better than when we came. We're a viable example that it's not only possible to pursue this alternative lifestyle, but that it's easy, dignifying and highly rewarding. To not share this with travelers would be greedy; to not share it with those devoted to carry this philosophy onward would be a great mistake and a huge loss.

Growing My Nerves

There are as many books on gardening as anyone could ever want; still I have yet to read one on how to deal with a gardener's weak nerves. There's no hiding it anymore – I'm a nervous-souled gardener. Some days I even find myself wishing, in secrecy, that the whole season would be over so I would know that everything went all right. The spring is so full of promise – promise of sun-ripe tomatoes, juicy strawberries, wonderful flower arrangements and sweet, sweet carrots. But so many obstacles lie between now and then – only when the harvest is secure in our cellar, in jars, boxes and on shelves will I know I outsmarted the slugs, kept ahead of the weeds and timed my actions with the sun, the rain and the frosts. Do I take it too seriously? Oh yes, but I believe I have reasons to. Our garden grows our food for the whole year. The monetary value of the produce is hard to estimate, and it's even harder to see that we would happily go to work outside our farm to make that money. Our economy, and therefore our life here, is closely tied to a successful garden.

My lack of experience definitely is a key factor in my fretting. A while back I planted hundreds of feet of carrots and it took almost a month for them to sprout. I went from hope to despair and back to hope again. Could it really be that all the seeds were bad? Was April too cold? Was it too dry, had I planted the seeds too deep or fried them in my generous doling out of compost? Anyone with more than a few years of doing this would know to wait patiently and it would all be all right.

My high ambitions might be what keep me going – I want every garden year to be the best across the whole range of crops – and that desire certainly keeps me on my feet. Sometimes people say things like, "Oh my God, look at your Brussels sprouts!" and I'm thinking, "Of course they look like that since I spent a full day hauling manure and turning it in, another day spreading seaweed, several mornings of being up at 4.30 am picking slugs and at least three nights awake wondering when to cut the tops."

There are so many decisions to make – when to start the tomato seeds, how many plants to grow, when to plant them outside and where to put them. And why do they have those wrinkled leaves, don't they seem a bit yellow, what if it doesn't rain at all in July and did we really have a cold enough winter to kill off the bugs? The thoughts are rolling over and over in my mind. I think of my old neighbor at our summer house in Sweden, the only farmer left in the village. How he walked the fields just as generations before him walked the fields, looking at the sky and the hay drying on the racks. Isn't that what they say? That for a farmer it's always too warm or too cold, too wet or too dry?

But maybe at the end of the day I am just a person with weak nerves doing something that depends on so many unknown factors – the weather, the bug population, the quality of the seeds and some plain ol' luck. Perhaps I can settle one day: I will have the experience, be better at managing my undertakings and I might even have grown stronger nerves. Perhaps I will have to eat fewer carrots some years but I still might get as many beets. I know the garden can be wonderful even with half the ambition, none of the worries and all of the sleep. I just need to learn how to cultivate that.

Natural Island Amendments for the Organic Garden

Summer solstice came and went with the typical cold and ambivalent weather, and June disappeared under our wet feet. All the plants I transplanted out in the garden a month ago are just about the same size now as they were then, sun-starved and pale, but alive.

When Dennis first came here 12 years ago, the driveway went straight through what's now one of our gardens. Until a few years ago, the other garden area still was a forest floor with standing trees. Now these areas are fertile gardens, created using the natural resources that are so abundant here on the island – from our yard, the forest, the shore and our neighbors' farms.

We never buy any amendments for our gardens or orchards. No matter how organic, the plastic bags, the obvious processing, the involvement of cash and the transport kinda' ruins the "natural" for me. Our goal is to use as much as we can from our own farm and after that go as short a distance as possible. We never have to go further than 5 miles to get what we need for the gardens and we attribute much of our gardening success, and by extension our ability for living with limited cash and a high level of food security, to the free resources around us.

The major island resource we use is the seaweed that washes up on the beaches here, generally considered one of the top amendments to use in a garden. In spring we use it as mulch around the plants to suppress weeds, add nutrients and keep the moisture in the ground. We plant our tomatoes by digging a hole, dumping a 5-gallon bucket of seaweed in it and planting the tomato right there. We add the seaweed to our compost piles, we put about a foot-thick ring of it around our fruit trees and we feed it to our chickens and to our pigs. In the fall as we harvest the produce we cover every bed with it for the winter. We get it by the trailer load and use as much as we can muster hauling in as many ways as we can think up.

We use oak leaves as mulch for crops that might be planted too close to lay down the bulky seaweed, such as leeks, for example. The leaves need to be shredded, and in preference to chickens over machines, throwing the leaves in the chicken pen not only takes care of the shredding and makes the chickens happy, but it also adds to the fertilization.

Instead of buying bales of straw, I bring home day lily leaves I cut back in the fall while doing landscaping and gardening around the island. Once again, I throw them in the chicken pen and after a few weeks they're ready to be used as mulch over our newly planted garlic. Corn stalks and corn leaves cut up and left to dry work just as well.

To lower the pH in our slightly acidic soil we spread about a quart of wood ash from our stove on each garden bed before planting.

As I have mentioned before, whenever we clean up brush around the yard and woods we stack it in long mounds at the edge of our clearing instead of burning it. Last summer we prepared a new building site and had to move the last residues of a brush pile made about a decade ago. Under a layer of remaining sticks was about a foot of wonderful, rich wood duff that we spread on our orchard.

We fertilize our fruit trees and flower beds with compost from our outhouses. We use a bucket and sawdust system and empty the content in simple pallet-bins and let it sit for a year before we break the piles open and use it. We use a separate bucket for urine, which after being diluted is an excellent source of nitrogen with which to water heavy feeding crops.

Every year we raise a couple of pigs that we feed largely from the same natural resources: the forest and the yard. Once we have butchered them and processed all the meat, we burn the bones until they are brittle and can be crushed into bonemeal and spread over our phosphorus-loving crops. From ashes to ashes, from the land to the land. There are always new ways to improve the soil, and a keen eye will be amazed how close and abundant the resources usually are.

Hosteling from Home

I haven't always been a homesteader on Deer Isle. Once I was a traveler, roaming the world looking for yet another untrodden path. My travels led me to different cultures, to war zones, deserts, mountains and oceans, usually on a very thin shoestring budget. I depended on cheap transport, inexpensive food and more than anything, budget accommodations. It was one of the determining factors for where my travels led me: if a place had a hostel, it was a place I could go to. Hostels made it possible for me to see the world and some of my fondest memories from traveling – as well as some of my best friends – come from hosteling. So a long time ago when I met Dennis (at a hostel) and was invited to help him start one in Maine, I didn't have to think twice.

Many people think of hostels as something from Europe. Our older visitors often tell us about trips they made overseas, staying at Youth Hostels, and many think of hostels as a place for bicyclists or hikers to stay. But times have changed and so have the hostels. Most have omitted the word "youth" and cater to people of all ages, with all kinds of transportation. Most hostels offer private rooms in addition to the traditional dorm rooms while keeping up with the signature communal kitchen, bathroom and living room.

We opened in 2009, and for those on a limited budget who don't want to travel with camping gear, or those who simply prefer the indoor option, we're their only choice in the area. In fact, we're the only hostel on the entire coast of Maine.

Many of our guests come with the Hostel as their destination and simply consider it luck that it happens to be located in such a beautiful place as Deer Isle. By now, we've seen travelers of all ages, from all continents and from all walks of life. Some come late and leave early. Some come by chance after seeing our road signs and end up coming back, year after year. One lady hasn't missed a single summer since we opened, and it's hard for me to imagine a summer without seeing the return of some of our guests. We've seen solo travelers congregate here by coincidence and leave as a group, friends have been made and plans to see each other back home hashed out.

And right now, just about this time every year our lives are changing. We're not just Dennis and Anneli living in a small cabin, spending our days together; we're host and hostess and we're spending our days with everyone. Last year we had about 250 guests, not counting all those who came for a tour, a workshop, an event or family members visiting. We make an effort to talk to them all. We put on a communal dinner for all of our guests every evening, and we try to catch most of them at breakfast before they leave. We long ago gave up trying to get bigger projects done in the summer months. New construction, landscaping or milling must wait until fall. In the summer we do laundry, we clean and we cook. I keep the gardens in shape and the bugs at bay, but mostly we socialize with our guests, point out bike routes, ATMs, restaurants and hiking trails. We assure them that they can make themselves at home and we hug most of them when they leave. In the afternoons I can go to my neighbor and take a nap on her lawn, at a safe ½ mile distance from the ringing phone. At the end of the season, I'm amazed I still remember my husband's name.

It makes me proud to run a hostel and to offer an affordable night's sleep on Deer Isle. It gives access to a beautiful, natural area and it might inspire others to live a more sustainable life. It's also a great way, mildly put, to keep life interesting. After about a decade of living in a backpack, jumping the hoops of visas and passports and border controls, and after spending night after night in new places, living on Deer Isle year round with the Hostel in full swing through the summer is the best of both worlds: the comfort of home with the vibrations of travelers.

Why We Raise Our Own Meat

One of the big events of the year took place the other day, when we brought our new piglets home. We bought them from a guy only a mile away, but the seemingly predictable event took a sudden turn when the 6-week-old little jokers bolted through the electric fence and disappeared into the woods as soon as we let them out. For about a week our neighbors kept us up-to-date on their whereabouts, either after seeing them galloping across their lawn or following the excitement on Facebook (posted by other neighbors and reported to us via phone). We kept a feed trough at the edge of our yard and eventually lured them in close enough to catch them. The adventurous pigs were named Louise and Clark.

For the next five months we will do all we can to keep them happy and comfortable: scratch their ears and their flanks, play with them, give them a big pen to roam in and a dry place to sleep. But the end is as clear as it's inevitable: no matter how much we love them, we still raise them for the meat.

There is nothing revolutionary about raising animals for meat; people have done that for thousands of years, nor is there anything new about killing the animals yourself either. What is new is the idea of meat production: raising animals in factory-like environments, transporting them hundreds of miles for slaughter, processing them on a conveyor belt and selling the meat from the freezer in a store. I don't eat store-bought meat at all because I want to know where the animal came from, how it lived and how its life ended. I want to know that once it was killed, as little waste as possible was created and the only way for us to be in control of it all is to do it ourselves.

Sometimes we get rather strong reactions when people understand why we have these animals around. Not only do we eat something so cute and loved, but we have the heart to kill it ourselves. Well trust me on this: I've had pets since I was old enough to babble out their names, I've trained horses and dogs and I've been a vegan, a vegetarian and everything in between and this kind of animal husbandry makes perfect sense to me. The fact is that these pigs would not be alive at all if they were not going to be eaten. The farmer who bred his sow and raised the litter would not have done that if not for people like us, who like to eat meat but don't want to buy it in the store. On a philosophical level, the reasoning that what we're doing is unethical raises the question if *no life* for our pigs would have been better than *this life*. Louise and Clark's lives will end on a cold November morning no different for them than any other cold November morning. Their death will be so sudden I can't imagine there's time for any thoughts or feelings, but just an end and nothing more. As a pig farmer, meat eater and animal lover, I believe that a happy and carefree life with an instant and painless end is indeed better than no life at all.

It might sound odd to care for and even love an animal when you know you soon will eat it, but we know it from day 1 and that makes a huge difference. By giving them names, attention and affection, we make life better for them and even if it's hard to think about the end, at least I know our pigs are the happiest pigs around for as long as they are around.

A Homesteader's Sense of Place

For the first 10 years after moving out of my parents' house, the longest I consecutively lived in one place was eight months. That place, as were most other places I called home, was in a big city where my needs were met in the office where I worked, the store where I bought my food and through the radiant heater that kept me warm. Now I think of myself as a homesteader, letting the land be my main provider of what I need.

To me homesteading creates a strong sense for, and connection to, the place I'm in. By working in the garden and the woods, I get to know the trees, the plants and the wildlife. I know the wet spots, the slopes, the shady areas and the sunny ones. By devoting my life to this particular place, I can recognize myself as a part of it and, by extension, to nature as a whole. I depend on water from the land the same way the trees and the deer do; and I depend on nutrients from the land the same way mushrooms and gold finches do. I'm not just an observer of nature but physically and spiritually a part of it.

A homesteader's life has a very tangible connection to the land: the carrots grow in the soil and I go to the garden to fetch them. The firewood, our source of heat, comes from the trees and the trees grow in the woods. The bacon is the pig in the pen. The eggs are in the chicken house. The sun makes the tomatoes grow and the rain waters the seeds. Logically, one who relies on nature ought also to care for nature.

Now as I'm making this journey down the homesteader's path, some things are so obvious I can't even imagine how I could have lived for so long having never thought about them – that the food in the store comes from a farm and that even the vegetables in a tin can once grew in the soil. I ate beans for 20 years before I saw a bean plant and I remember how amazed I was when I first saw a real-life pear tree. Food came from the store, period, and nature was something I could visit on weekends.

Other connections also now have become clear: that fossil fuels used to run cars and produce plastic materials come from the earth, and the metal used in electronic gadgets comes from the earth too, as does the asphalt on the roads and the rubber in my bike tires. It all comes from the earth, and too often nature pays a high price when these resources are extracted.

During the last century fewer and fewer people have been living with a hands-on connection to the source of their sustenance and that seems to have created a gap in our relation to nature. One example of the consequences is global warming, that to me is not a climate problem but rather a spiritual problem created by this disconnection. For many, what happens in, or to, the environment – like severe changes in weather patterns – simply doesn't happen to them.

Encouraging a re-establishment of the connection between individuals and nature could perhaps reverse this trend. To teach people that the food on their plates comes from the soil and that the fuel in their cars comes from the ground, at nature's expense, and that no green windows or hybrid cars can replace a true connection to the natural world around them. The changing climate shouldn't be a nature vs. people issue. We need to look at the trees, the stones, the animals and the sky and realize that we are all nature and nature is us. Everything surrounding us comes from the ground, and we too come from the soil, the very same soil, and we will all – humans, rabbits, mosses, day lilies and oak leaves alike – return to it. When we as individual human beings truly identify ourselves with every living organism out there and fully appreciate where our sustenance for living comes from, that's when we also truly will have a chance of lessening the impact on and making peace with nature.

The Hostel Homesteader's August

 Suddenly, as if we've been transported in time, we are half-way through August and the summer won't last forever anymore but only for a few more weeks. As always, I don't know how it happened, where it went or where the first signs of fall came from. All I know is that suddenly the peak of the season is upon us and ahead is a slow winding road to the silent winter.

 I've spent days thinking about this blog entry and what to write – something that's on my mind, something interesting, perhaps educational, slightly radical. But what's on my mind can best be described visually, by a flat hand held an inch from my face: all I can think of is what is right here right now. The pig pen needs to be moved and if it's sunny tomorrow I can paint the corner boards of the chicken house. I have to remember to check the Brassicas for caterpillars, remember to pick the onions soon, clean up the garlic, pick the Shiitakes, bag them, sell them. We have our big FarmFeast dinner event next Saturday: I don't have plates, I don't have a musician, I have a car with a hole in the gas tank to fetch the 10 tables and 30 chairs. Four days from now I'm giving a workshop in organic gardening that I remember only thanks to the ads someone else posted. I have another slightly major undertaking three weeks from now that I should start worrying about. But what's the point? My hand is already so close to my face I can't see beyond it.

 The summer doesn't so much slip through my fingers as it escapes me with a wild roar. I've already seen the signs: the first yellow leaves, the golden rods, the steam from my mouth one early morning. Sure, there are still summer-ripe peaches to eat and my annual swim across the pond and there are still a number of guests whose presence we'll enjoy. Nevertheless, I don't know where the summer went or where it's going after leaving, all I know is that the road will end in winter and I'd be lying if I said I haven't enjoyed it just as I'd be lying if I said I didn't long for fall.

Homesteading Economics 103

As children we all got asked what we wanted to be when we grew up. I, as most of my peers, grew up with parents working full time who disappeared early and came home late. A profession, and having a job to go to, is part of one's identity, of who you are and what you're doing with your life.

As I've mentioned before, Dennis and I prefer not to have an off-the-farm job to go to, at least not more than once in a great while. We like to spend our days at home, together, and make what we need right here, from our land. That's what both my parents – and generations before them – did too, one in the woods and one on a farm, before moving to the city and being away at work every day. Mum often recalls the pleasure of her family being able to set their daily schedule, to stop for coffee when the neighbor came by and how they all worked in the fields together. But as if this was something only from the past, no one ever presented this lifestyle as an option to me growing up.

A way of living where gains are earned through physical labor, practical skills and devotion to a place has largely been replaced in modern Western society by a way of living where gains are made by financial strategies and depletion of resources, all without almost any physical or spiritual connection to the place or the people involved.

For many, having a job to go to is a way to feel a sense of belonging and a way of being respected for one's skills and experience. It can be a way to contribute not only to the household budget, but to the community.

But often when I hear politicians and economists talk about the perceived necessity of going to work, or as they say, being a part of "the work-force," it's usually referred to as a way to contribute to a growing economy. That growth will happen when people have a salary they can spend buying a bigger house, another car or a new TV. That kind of spending will supposedly lead to more people getting a job and enjoying the same benefits (more money). Supposedly, this growing economy will increase our freedom and make us happier.

Well, I've never been able to put this logic together. I don't see how a growing economy will give us, or this planet, what we need. To say that people should work – regardless of the conditions, the salary or possibilities for personal and spiritual growth – for the sake of such vague goals as "a strong consumer economy" and "profit margins" is to reduce the individual person into a disposable part in a system where advantages made at the expense of others are not only accepted, but expected. To stress the importance of increased consumerism is to ignore the environmental impacts that such an economy has and to encourage a system that heedlessly abuses local and global resources, as if no one and nothing depended on them.

But I often also hear another story, one about down-scaling. The CEO who quit his job and became a lock-smith, or the hotel manager that started a three-day-a-week bakery. People who listened to the talk about the growing economy and realized that it was nothing but a lie: they already had all that money could buy and still didn't experience freedom, or happiness. They down-scaled, stopped, drew the line, went back to the source or back to the land. I dare to say I'm not the only one rejecting the idea of limitless growth – I think we're heading into a hopeful future where less will be more. A sense of belonging, respect and contributing can be achieved in many ways – as a community volunteer or as an engaged member of a family or a neighborhood, for example – without taking part in what I consider a very destructive part of our society. Money enough to secure basic needs is one thing, but after that money brings excess, not joy.

When telling others about how and why we live as we do, it seems as if more and more people recognize the merits of living in simplicity and that to care for one's home and land is not something left behind from the past but rather a sensible, dignifying and viable option for the future.

If You Can Keep It
You Can Eat It: Part 1

I'm in the beginning of the second big push of the gardening year: the processing. All those plants I've worked so hard to grow have indeed been growing, and as the Hostel season now wraps up and I thought I would have a break, the cabbages, the broccoli – the whole garden, in unison – started to call for attention. Since my ambition is to eat year round from a garden that for a good part of the year is covered in snow, I need to make sure that I both grow enough quantity to last through the year and I better figure out how to preserve and store it. I have no interest in selling my produce in August only to buy the same products from Canada or California in March. We don't have a freezer, so learning other ways of keeping our food through the whole year has been a key element in our journey to the high level of food self-sufficiency we now enjoy.

Starting millennia ago with mead, fermentation is the oldest known way humans have preserved food and beverages. All across the globe people for centuries have used the ever-existing live culture yeasts and microorganisms to preserve vegetables, cheese, grain and meat as well as to produce wine, coffee and chocolate. Perhaps the most well-known source of information about fermenting food is *Wild Fermentation* by Sandor Ellix Katz, and for those who really want to geek out he also wrote *The Art of Fermentation*.

I got my first sauerkraut lesson many years ago and discovered it was as simple as shredding the cabbage and adding salt. How much salt? Just sprinkle it in as you go. Crush the cabbage with your hands to draw out the liquid, pack it snugly in a vessel and keep it submerged. Add ginger and hot pepper and it's a South Korean dish called Kim-Chi. Wait a few days and eat it.

Today fermentation is one of my primary ways of preserving our produce. I grow hundreds of heads of cabbage each season, many of which we store fresh and many of which are turned into around 30 gallons of kraut per year. Once we get going, we eat almost one of those gallons a week, along with a selection of the 80-100 quarts of fermented beans, cucumbers, broccoli, Brussels sprouts and salsa I also squeeze into our well-stocked cellar.

I took to fermentation not only because of the vast health and flavor benefits it brings with it, but largely because for me, it's the ultimate self-sufficient way of preserving food. By packing the produce in a simple salt and water brine I can safely keep such vegetables as broccoli and green beans through the winter, and I can preserve damaged vegetables such as cracked heads of cabbage or carrots the voles have munched on. There is no freezer involved, thus no power grid. There is no cooking or heating involved, thus no fuel expended. I get my gallon jars from a restaurant down the road that otherwise would throw them in the dumpster, and I can reuse them year after year. Fermentation is self-sufficiency, and self-sufficiency is a political agenda: by growing, preserving and eating our own food, I can stay away from the highly unsustainable and harmful food industry, the fossil fuel-based agriculture and the massive logistics involved in transporting the food. By providing for ourselves, we are no longer limited to the food quality and diversity others make available.

With my organic gardens, the fermentation vessels and our root cellar I have been able to move the most basic of our needs, eating, from the hands of corporations (food, oil, stores) to the hands of myself. Planting, tending, harvesting and eventually packing the salted cabbage, beans or mixed salsa in jars is the ultimate hands-on political action I can think of. And it comes with a reward: summer preserved, all year.

Succession Planting for Space Saving and Season Extension

The Hostel has been closed for about a week. We made it through the summer in style, but we're in great need for some quiet time to decompress. It's time to go back to being just Dennis and me and the homestead.

My fourth year ever as a gardener brought the coldest June, the hottest July, a rainy August. What can I say? There are unknown cards in every hand, but one has to make the most of it. The learning opportunities and chances to improve are as endless as the changing weather forecasts.

Each year I seem to improve some in one way or another, and this year has not been an exception. Our tomato vines usually grow six feet tall, so finally I scrapped the flimsy tomato cages and put the plants along the fence where they easily could be tied up. Last year's infestation of cucumber beetles took me by surprise, but this year we started to patrol our plants long before any damaged could happen. But why oh why did I plant basil where it would be shaded by the pepper plants, and why on earth did I grow my beans where they would be such easy prey for the slugs? But life is forgiving to dedicated gardeners, always giving us another season to correct our mistakes.

It's mid-September; the first leaves have fallen and the grass is slowly turning brown. The pond is getting too cold to swim in. Still, we are only in the middle of the gardening season. For a few years my focus has been on expanding the footprint of the garden; now I'm improving the ways to make the most of what I have. Even as far north as Maine I can harvest produce from March to December, with parsnips to dig from under February's frost, without the use of row covers or a greenhouse. A Maine summer is as short as it is sweet and plants such as tomatoes and peppers already are compromised. In late August I cut their tops off and snip off all flowers so the plants will put their energy into finishing what's already there rather than forming new fruit that won't have time to mature. Last year I cut the tops of the Brussels sprouts to encourage less top-growth and ended up with golf-ball-sized sprouts.

Some crops have already been harvested. In previous years we just mulched those beds with seaweed and called it good, while this year I thought I should make use of that now available space. In early July I planted rutabagas and a 52-day variety of Chinese cabbage in the plots that opened up after our early lettuce bolted. A few weeks later I transplanted those seedlings to the beds from where I had just picked our garlic. In August we picked the onions and the early potatoes and quickly filled the new space with rows of short, cool weather crops like radish, spinach and turnips. All these will mature and be picked before winter – the Chinese cabbage "replanted" in boxes with damp sawdust and kept in the root cellar, the radishes turned into colorful ferments and the turnips baked each night in the oven, sweet enough to call dessert. In a few weeks it's already time to start thinking about next spring. I'll get my wooden cold frames out and plant kale and spinach that will overwinter and be ready to pick – probably at the same time as we start to run low on cabbage in the cellar – in a still distant early spring.

Apple Abundance as a
Part of Our History

We are enjoying an absolutely fantastic fall here on Deer Isle and we are quickly carried away with new endeavors. One of many projects around our farm this fall is to clear ground for where we will plant ten apple trees next spring. There's drainage to work on, brambles to fight and brush to move. The apple trees, now growing in our vegetable garden, are still only a couple of feet tall and thin as whips. It takes a great leap of imagination to believe that these little sticks in a couple of decades will be stout, apple-laden trees growing in a place that right now looks like a bomb went off.

The first basic thing to know about apples is that with a few exceptions, they don't come true from seed. That means that if you plant a seed from a Red Delicious, the tree growing from that seed won't produce Red Delicious apples but rather its own, unique apple variety, unlike any apple there ever was. To get a Red Delicious, you will have to graft. Grafting is a whole subject on its own, but basically it means taking a few inches long piece of new-growth wood with 3 to 4 buds – this is called a scion – from the tree you like to propagate and joining that scion onto an existing tree or rootstock and letting them grow together. Everything growing from that scion will be the same variety as the tree from which you cut it. Apple trees grown from seeds – planted either intentionally or discarded by people or animals – are usually referred to as seedlings, and the variety doesn't have a name. Before breeding programs for apples were invented, all apple varieties started as one wild seedling tree. Someone found the tree along the road or in the woods, tried the fruit and liked it, cut a scion, grafted it, named it and from there on it spread.

From Maine to Georgia and west to the Mississippi river, there used to be about 15,000-20,000 grafted apple varieties. Most every farm and homestead had some trees that they cared for, whether they were used only for the household or as a part of a diversified income. Many villages, neighborhoods and towns had their unique apple trees named after a person or a location. People knew how to best enjoy the different varieties: not all apples meet their peak performance when eaten fresh. Some taste best in a pie, others as sauce and some taste best in February after being kept in the cellar. The orchards were planned after the intended uses for the apples.

Today, when commercialism is king and the most known apple varieties are the five kinds offered in the supermarkets, those old varieties are worth paying attention to. One of the most interesting agriculture projects in Maine right now is the heritage orchard that is being established in Unity, Maine, by the Maine Organic Farmers and Gardeners Association. Some 500 old varieties of apples and pears are being planted as a way to preserve Maine's legacy as a great apple state. As with all things around us, diversity is interesting and sustainable. There are trees in our immediate neighborhood that are around 150-160 years old. There are varieties on this island that were once loved and cared for, trees that had fantastic pie apples or that turned the cider into champagne, varieties that kept until May in the cellar. There are trees that someone named after his wife or son or the cove they lived by, varieties where now perhaps only one single tree remains. By learning about identification and grafting that tree can be replanted and saved as a part of our history and heritage.

If You Can Keep It
You Can Eat It: Part 2

If I ever were to build another place to live, the first thing I'd consider would be the root cellar, or an equivalent space that naturally would stay cold enough to store food. I can't emphasize enough the importance of low-energy food storage: the ability to keep food without a freezer, refrigerator, fuel-consuming processing or artificially cold rooms (cold-bot controlled) is for me a key to self-sufficiency. Fermentation is one way to give food a longer storing capacity, but many crops can be kept fresh all the way to next summer if kept in the right way. For the past few years we have tried different ways of storing fresh food, and now we are eating garlic, onions, squash, carrots, rutabagas and beets until June, and usually we run out of our supply before it goes bad. By fall-planting greens in cold frames for an early spring harvest and by planting short-seasoned varieties of for example carrots, we now overlap many crops from one year to the next.

Any place with the right temperature and the right moisture can be used to store food. Most root crops require a temperature around mid to low 30° F, without freezing. If the cellar isn't the right place, perhaps the garage will work, or the mudroom. Also, one can make do with a north facing bulkhead by opening and closing the door to control the temperature.

Different varieties of the same crop keep differently. Onions, for example, have sweeter varieties with a limited storage life and varieties that are denser and more pungent with excellent keeping properties. When planning our gardens in the spring I prioritize the keeping varieties by, for example, planting fewer summer squash that ripens when everything ripens and more winter squash that we can enjoy into late spring.

We pack our carrots, beets, rutabagas and celeriac in wooden boxes with damp spruce sawdust. We built the boxes uniformly so that we can stack them and keep out the rodents. The boxes also were measured to fit mason jars. The damp sawdust not only keep the produce moist, it also stays cooler than the room temperature, so in the spring when our cellar quickly gets too warm, the root crops are cold and snug in their boxes.

We store our cabbage in the same way but in much bigger boxes. I pick the cabbage by pulling it up with the root and cleaning off several layers of outer leaves. The biggest challenge with cabbage is to not let worms or slugs remain between the leaves since they will spoil the produce. The leaves that we do end up removing can be fermented whole in crocks and served as leafy tortilla wraps. The Chinese cabbages get picked the same way, but we "replant" them in sawdust just the same way they sat in the ground. A deeper box may be flipped over the heads to keep the light and rodents out.

Onions, garlic and leeks all spend the winter in our mudroom where it stays cold and much drier than in the cellar. The winter squash want to be warm (60-70°F) and dry so they hang out in our former sleeping loft where we no longer can fit a bed among all the pumpkins. We store several bushels of fresh apples and pears in our mudroom. A good fresh storage fruit has no bruises (picked from the tree and handled carefully), has the stem left on and no signs of bugs. The fruit that doesn't meet those requirements we store as sauce or we dry them on screens over our wood stove. Cider is an excellent way of using apples that have too much damage to be good for any other purpose. Read up about how to make it and invite friends for pressing parties and taste trials! Blueberries, cranberries, strawberries and rhubarb I turn into sauce and preserve it with traditional canning methods, to the tune of 100+ pints every year.

And how about the parsnips? Well, those we keep right where they are, in the ground. As their tops die back in the fall we cover them with mulch and leave them. Around February or so, just as we begin to crave some variety to our meals, the ground usually thaws out just enough for me to go out and fork off big sheets of frozen seaweed and dirt and dig out the buttery-sugary, crisp and cold parsnips.

If you can keep it you can eat it, anytime.

Feeding Pigs From Our Land

I had a gray morning today. The sky was gray, the water was gray and the garden looked gray. I was left alone at home, unmotivated and weary. I walked out to the pig pen and called for Louise and Clark. After a few calls I could see the pigs running through the tall brush, coming down the slope to the stream and surprisingly vigorously for their size jumping over a log and trotting up the slop towards me. To see these pigs come when I call for them never fails to lift my spirit.

We let our pigs run in the woods not only because they look so much in their element, having all this land to roam in and feed from, but because we would like to extend our high level of self-sufficiency to the feeding of our pigs. It's one of the biggest challenges we face: to progress away from a grain diet and supply the majority of the pig feed from our land. We certainly have made strides, but it's a work in progress.

The common practice of feeding livestock commercial grain (including what's labeled organic) is both unnatural to the animals and a very new practice compared the many centuries people raised animals without grain. Animal grain relies on fossil fuel for growing the feed crops, for the production and the distribution logistics. The price fluxes with the price of the commodities used in the manufacturing process, and have over the past years gone through a heavy increase. Farmers we know that raise animals on grain say that due to that increase they have to work harder for the same gains now compared to some years ago.

For the first couple of years that we raised pigs, we kept them in a small mobile pen within the clearing of our farm and fed them mostly grain. Even though we often moved them to new ground, the pigs quickly wore it out by rooting. Now we keep the pigs penned in our yard only when they are small, to get them used to us and to keep them safe from the coyotes. As soon as they are big enough, we use our entire supply of electric wire to make a large pen out in the woods, with only a small section of it within sight of our house. For most of the day our pigs run like wild ponies around the spruce trees and oak trees, digging up roots and rocks, eating acorns and spruce cones and moss and dirt, and surely some toads and salamanders too. I can tell from one day to the next that if I feed them a big grain breakfast in the morning, they will stay in their house until I come back with the bucket. But if I cut back on the feed, I can go out and watch them gnawing on roots and chewing on brambles leaves. Pigs are scavengers and have evolved to fend for themselves – to forage for food and to be hungry from time to time. We supplement their forest floor diet with seaweed, corn stalks and the Chinese cabbage that at the end of harvest season has failed to grow big enough for us to bother with. When we're out picking apples we always bring bags with us to collect the wind-blown fruit, and in a good year that amounts to a substantial part of the pigs' diet.

Feeding acorns and surplus apples to pigs is a way to convert a land resource into a high-grade food for human consumption, and especially into fats, which are hard to find in nature where we live.

After four years of raising pigs and butchering them ourselves I can't see any correlation between their size and the amount of grain they were fed. The pig we raised that was the biggest and had the greatest amount of fat was the pig fed the least grain in a poor acorn year that left a very lean diet to forage. Rather it turns out to be the breed that largely determines the size and fat proportions. Dennis and I clearly prefer heritage breeds, which are easy to raise to a good size on backyard resources.

Our pig pen in the woods not only means higher independence from external sources, such as the grain and oil industries, but it also means less destroyed ground around the farm, healthier and better tasting meat and a huge financial gain. But mostly, it means a great feeling of pride and joy seeing what a good life our dear animals have.

Homesteading Economics 104;
The Future

Not long ago I woke up in the middle of the night with words from the radio news ringing in my ears. Debt ceiling, default, melt down. "If this is *it*," I thought, turning in bed and trying to think clearly, "and the economy really is going to hit the fan, where is our security?" Later, in the clarity of the morning light, I calmed down and could see exactly where: it's right here in our land, our gardens and in our manual labor skills.

Homesteading is an excellent way to live in independence and self-reliance. When Dennis and I look ahead to see how we can provide for ourselves 10, 20 and even 30 years from now, homesteading seems perhaps even more as a realistic lifestyle. It's generally assumed and widely accepted that cheap fossil fuels won't pave the way much longer for goods, food and materials from all over the world. Some things that are now taken for granted probably won't be as abundant if they will be available at all. Most people's means of making a living and providing for their needs will change dramatically within a few decades, and fending for oneself might not only be an option but a necessity.

The Hostel is our "cash crop" now and even though people might cut back on their vacation travels, many are more likely to choose a budget option for lodging if they do venture out. We already notice a surge to learn homesteading and self-sufficiency skills, and our guess is that that will only increase. And even if it turns out to be but an ill-conceived assumption that the Hostel will keep supporting us, we already live a pretty secure, low-cash kind of life.

My thoughts about our future economy aren't so much what to change, but rather to stay on track: to stay away from fuel-intensive endeavors such as heated greenhouses, farming that involves machinery or livestock that require heated spaces, butchering facilities and grain feed. I won't get a freezer or hook up to the grid and risk losing that constant strive we now have for developing the skills and creativity it takes to get by without. By moving away from fossil fuel dependency, we won't be as easily hurt when it becomes less available.

The orchard we're breaking ground for is a part of our future economic plan. Apples as a part of a diversified economy can be a worthwhile investment to make now, if (when) fruit from California or Argentina won't be as cheap and readily available as they are today. Some nut trees take a long time to mature but could turn out to be of great significance for filling the oil and protein slot in our diet or as a cash crop. Land is another investment we consider: it could be used to expand the farm or the Hostel, to feed animals on or as a source of firewood and building materials. It also generally increases in value, in case we have an unforeseen need for cash (emergency healthcare, for example).

Homesteading skills may be just as valuable for a secure future, perhaps more so, as any material assets. It's a great comfort for us to have experience in growing and storing food and it's also a comfort to know how to build shelters, fix things, raise animals, forage wild edibles and any number of other such abilities.

It's not my intention to paint a bleak picture of the future. Rather, I think a future with more homesteading, more small farming and food production projects and a better utilization of backyard resources sounds like a great improvement! I also believe that there never is a better time or place to start preparing for that future than right now and right here.

The Love of Local Food
(as in a few-yards-away kind of local)

The first morning with hard frost is a sure sign of the changing seasons. From one day to the next it's like walking out to a whole different garden: the dead bean vines, the morning glory that hangs like a black ghost on the fence and the red kale that has now turned purple. Fall is here with no looking back, and we're in the midst of our big harvest. For a few remarkable weeks all four seasons will be represented daily on our dinner plates: summer tomatoes that still ripen on our window sill, radishes as in the spring, winter Brussels sprouts sweetened off by that shimmering frost and fall in the shape of pumpkins, cabbages.

While it's true that I like gardening, more than that, I like eating. I like to work hard and get hungry and then think about what to snack on, I like to wake up and dream up a breakfast before leaving bed and I love talking about food: what someone ate last night, what Dennis had for lunch if I wasn't around, what others plan for dinner. The few days I go to work somewhere else I spend an ocean of time preparing a lunch box, an afternoon snack and deciding what kind of apple to bring. I plan meals days in advance and I rarely cook a dinner with less than three dishes, even on an ordinary Tuesday. I appreciate abundance; such is my indulgence that if eating fresh, homegrown produce could be considered sinful, my only saving grace would be all the hard work I had to perform to get it to my kitchen.

One thing that gardening has done for me, as it probably has for so many others, is that I've started to pay attention to where the food on my plate comes from, and usually the answer is "from our garden". As a consequence, I now tend to avoid food where the answer isn't as straight forward, or where the list of ingredients more resembles a chemistry quiz than food items. When sitting down for a meal, I like to imagine the plot where the vegetables grew, the field of wheat or rice and the chickens in their pen. It's a way to acknowledge that food doesn't come from "the store" or "the factory," but from the land, whether it's our land or somebody else's land. I couldn't do this if my mental image supply didn't include a picture of a tomato plant, a cucumber vine, a cabbage head. Before I grew a garden on my own, I never asked myself where food came from. And even if I had, what would the answer have been? I had never seen a tomato plant, a cucumber vine or a cabbage head in the ground. I remember the first time I saw a broccoli plant, well into my 20s. I remember it so clearly that I didn't even shrug when someone mistook our 9-foot sunflower (!) for a broccoli plant this past summer. It could have been me, a few years ago.

One way to appreciate food is to let it take as long to eat the meal as it did to cook it. Another way to appreciate home-grown food is to contemplate the hands-on labor – and sometimes sheer luck – it took to make it happen. Our tomato seedlings are started and for the first couple of months raised on our kitchen table. Every day we carry the 15 or so trays out in the sunshine and back in again at night. One cold April evening they were left outside and I had to leave a dinner party early to save them. They also magically survived a notoriously cold and wet June as well as horn worms and fruit flies. I think of this as I cut one up: all the luck and labor that brought this tomato into my kitchen. Last year the beetles took all our cucumbers, but this year we got as many as we could handle and I gave my thanks for each and every one of them.

Another thing gardening has done is to give me a genuine appreciation for fresh, healthy food. Or maybe it was the appreciation I already had for fresh, healthy food that gave me a genuine desire for growing such food myself. No matter how it started, it came to this: that I can sit down with my plate and all that's on it comes from no further than 50 yards away: my own gardens.

Off the Grid
with Solar Power

For the first few years Dennis lived here, he lived without electricity. As the Hostel started to materialize, the impracticality and hazards with candles and lanterns pushed him to set up a power system. The cost of running the grid line in from the road was too steep and the poles unsightly in the rustic setting, so Dennis set up a solar electric system. The system has grown some since, but it still is our only source of power, giving us enough electricity for light bulbs, a computer and on sunny days: the laundry machine, the water pump for the shower and some occasional power tools.

To live with alternative household energy in part or in full, as we are, is not so much a choice of energy source but as a choice of energy consumption. While it's possible to live off the grid – with solar power, for example – and still generate as much electricity as a conventional household consumes, I appreciate the limitations our fairly small set-up has. Those wishing to reduce their use of conventional power often consider renewable energy, but using laundry lines instead of a dryer is also a way to reduce power usage, as is reconsidering the necessity of other household appliances.

There's a common notion throughout society that we should all do what we can to halt global warming but that we should be able to do that without having to sacrifice anything; that while it's our duty to save the environment, it's our human right to keep using all the modern technology, appliances and devices we want. Renewable energy is often seen as a way to have it all and still feel "green". Indeed, at first glance, it is more environmentally friendly than conventional, nonrenewable power, but no power has as low footprint as the power not used.

It took energy – probably conventional – to produce the appliances that run on green energy. It will take energy to deal with them once they have been replaced, which, once again, probably will be conventional. Solar panels and wind turbines take energy to manufacture, batteries require large amounts of lead and hydro power comes with other environmental challenges.

Living off the grid with a stand-alone solar power system the way we do, is a great way to encourage a limitation of power usage. I don't ever miss having a refrigerator or other kitchen appliances, and aesthetically I appreciate the lack of such. I'm happy to adjust to the circumstances, that there are things we can do on sunny days that we cannot do on cloudy days. We don't have to consider a monthly payment to the power company and a well-designed solar electric system is substantially more reliable than the grid. A system like ours makes it possible to live, with electricity, on land too far away from the grid to bring the lines in, land that is often cheap and secluded.

The November days are getting shorter and we are enjoying the long evenings powered by the generously sunny days. We harvested the beets last Monday in the nick of time before the first real cold came. That was the end of the harvest season, an end that seemed so far away for so long that I still can't really believe we're on the other side of it.

Old Ways of Processing Pork at Home

Although I don't actively practice any religion, minutes before our pigs were killed this past Friday I did seek peace and comfort in the one prayer I know – probably mostly for my own sake: I needed consolation, they just wanted breakfast.

We kill our pigs right in their pen. With the right kind of gun and confident aim we ensure an instant and painless death without hours of transport and fear. We also stay in control of processing the meat and we can use the odd bits that otherwise would go to waste. Like the brain, for example, that we fry up and spread on bread, or the heart, that fried and served with vegetables is big enough for several meals.

We shoot each pig between the eyes and cut its throat to bleed it out. Once dead, we attach a gambrel to the tendons by the pig's rear hoofs. With a rope and pulley we hoist the animal up and lower it into a barrel with steaming (160°F) water to scald the skin so we can scrape off the hair. Usually the pig is too big to be submerged, so after dipping and scraping the front half, we attach a hook in its lower jaw, hoist it up and dip the rear half. Once it's clean we cut the head off and hoist the animal up again to take out the guts and then we hand saw it in half from top to bottom.

We use some old tried and true techniques for how to process the meat so it will keep without being put in a freezer. The hams, shoulders, bacon, back fat, tenderloin and loin, along with the jowls and the trotters (feet), we rub down with a sugar and salt (1:4) mix to cure and preserve them. We keep the pieces in plastic tubs and as water drains from the meat and accumulates in the tub, we empty it out to keep the meat as dry as possible. Since the hams are so thick, they are the hardest cuts to dry. We put weights (a board and some bricks) on them to press out even more liquid. In a few weeks we get our smoke house going to seal the cure and add flavor by smoking them.

Not too long ago in the Western world, livestock was too valuable not to use every bit of it, and this is still true in many parts of the world. It's inevitable that some of the animal will end up buried in our garden or as bonemeal fertilizer from charred and crushed bones or boiled down and fed to the chickens. But we constantly strive to learn new, mostly old, ways of utilizing and preserving more of the pigs for our own consumption.

Headcheese has nothing to do with cheese, but it's usually enjoyed the same way, on crackers or bread. We make it by cleaning the head (removing eyes and ears) and boiling the meat off the bones together with the tongue. Once tender and well broken down, the meat is packed in jars or molds and covered with the gelatinous broth created while cooking. We also make *confit*, which is an excellent way to use the small bits of meat that accumulate while cleaning up bigger cuts. We chop the meat fine and put it in a Dutch oven with rendered lard and let it boil for a long time until all the water is gone. The mix is put in jars, cooled and then covered with a layer of fat as a preservative. Both the headcheese and the *confit* we keep in our root cellar during the winter. We make soup stock by thoroughly boiling off any small bits of meat from the bones, and we render the fat to make lard that we use as cooking grease, skin lotion and to rub down our leather boots and mittens.

Still, we have much left to learn. The liver is a substantial part of the pig that could be processed and eaten, and the blood could be used for blood pudding and blood sausage. We'll try our hands at salami one of these years and we have already saved the ears and the tail for further processing and fearless eating experiences.

There no longer are a Louise and Clark, at least not out in the pen. Our pigs become a part of our lives and daily routines and even though we know the end will come, we're still poorly prepared for how strangely deserted the yard suddenly feels. But to say that the pigs are gone is an ill-conceived statement: our pigs will live on, through us, in the many abundant meals they provide.

Winter on Deer Isle

A few weeks have passed since we marked the end of the homesteading year by butchering our pigs. The gardens had all been taken care of at that point and the fall chores wrapped up. Today the first snow storm is upon us.

From a distance, say Maryland or Florida or any other place where most of the summer people on Deer Isle reside at this time of the year, winter here probably seems pretty rough. The snowed-in roads, the empty storefronts, the wind. The silence. All which are good reasons for the rest of us to stay, as is the diminished traffic, the snow-heavy spruce branches and the indisputable end to a long, hectic season. Pretty frequently I'm asked by our Hostel guests what we do here in the winter. I take it as a sign that our life must seem different from most people's lives, or at least seem to lack obvious forms of entertainment. Well, winter on Deer Isle is great, so great I consider it something we deserve after getting through the summer, both for us as homesteaders and for us as a part of this community.

Our daily routines are different in the winter. Maybe we get out of the house at 8 am, maybe at 9 am. Maybe we work until noon and stay inside the rest of the day, maybe we work the whole day. Playing hooky is fun after months and months of doing only what should have been done yesterday. Now we can do things of lesser importance, like cleaning up brush in the woods even though it's not absolutely necessary, or taking long walks to look at animal tracks in the snow. We can spend a whole Saturday taking baths by the wood stove and have the phone unplugged by mistake for two days and not even notice.

I've learned how to knit and quilt and make fabric collages, I'm writing blogs and letters and plowing through books. I make notes to remember good radio shows that I can enjoy with a glass of wine. I sleep. If I ever get bored I think about August and how I so often in the summer wish I had time to get bored, and then I soon feel better.

While there is no end to the activities and events on the island in summer, we who live here year round are usually too busy to show up unless we're arranging it. Now, after a few months of decompressing, we are all ready to socialize again. Winter can be pretty busy, if one's O.K. with simple things. Like the library that's open on Monday evenings where we not only can check out books and magazines but also can catch up with friends and neighbors and the latest talk of the town. Or the movies at the Stonington Opera House, that sometimes are such social gatherings that the actual movie when it begins feels more like an interruption than the event. Here, as in most small communities, people aren't spoiled by venues providing the entertainment. Here we do it ourselves: cribbage tournaments, ugly sweater parties, storytelling nights, ice skating and cross country skiing. Potlucks, Christmas caroling, and, to top it all off: a grand New Year's sledding party, complete with hot coco, chili and a bonfire.

Ahead is Christmas, my winter visit to Sweden and the project of building a little hut for myself where I can withdraw at the end of the Hostel evenings next summer.

A homesteader's year is over for this time. Nothing cleans the yard up as the first winter storm does. See you on the other side of the mounding snow.